Canada Close Up

Quebec

Marguerite Rodger

Scholastic Canada Ltd.
Toronto New York London Auckland Sydney
Mexico City New Delhi Hong Kong Buenos Aires

Visual Credits

Cover: Michael Turner/Team Turner Photography; p. I: Pete Ryan/National Geographic Stock; p. III: Yves Marcoux/First Light; p. IV: Andrew Barker/Shutterstock Inc. (right), Digital Vision/First Light (left); p. 2 and back cover: Yves Marcoux/First Light; p. 3: Bryan & Cherry Alexander Photography/Alamy (top), Gavriel Jecan/A.G.E. Fotostock/First Light (bottom); p. 5: Bruce Corbett/Alamy; pp. 6-7: David Giral/Alamy; p. 8: Pete Ryan/National Geographic Image Collection; p. 9: Yves Marcoux/First Light (top), Publiphoto Diffusion Inc/Alamy (bottom); p. 10: Guido Cozzi/Corbis; p. 11: Michelle Hagar; p. 12: Rolf Hicker/A.G.E. Foto Stock/First Light; p. 13: Christopher J. Morris/Corbis; p. 14: Library and Archives Canada, Acc. No. 1991-35-3; p. 15: David R. Frazier Photolibrary, Inc./Alamy; p. 16: The London Art Archive /Alamy; pp. 18-19: Library and Archives Canada, Acc. No. 1989-401-3; p. 20: Stapleton Collection/Corbis; p. 22: Library and Archives Canada, Acc. No. 1990-215-24R; p. 23: Mark Henley/Panos Pictures; p. 25: CP Picture Archive/Montreal Star; p. 26: Earl & Nazima Kowall/Corbis; p. 27: NASA/Alamy; p. 28: Howard Sandler/Shutterstock Inc.; p. 29: First Light; p. 30: Bryan & Cherry Alexander Photography/Alamy; p. 31: Jeff Greenberg/Alamy; p. 32: Creatas/First Light; p. 33: Richard Levine/Alamy (top), Michael DeFreitas North America/Alamy (bottom right); Picture Arts/First Light (bottom left); p. 34: AFP/Getty Images; p. 35: Reuters/Toby Melville; p. 36: CP Photo/Ian Barrett; p. 37: Hemis/Corbis (top), CP Photo/Saguenay Le Quotidien - Michel Tremblay (bottom); p. 38: Jupiter Images/Alamy; p. 39: CP Photo; p. 41: Philippe Renault/First Light (bottom), Egmont Strigl/Alamy (top); p. 42: Reuters/Joe Skipper (middle), Toronto Star/First Light (bottom), Bruce Weaver/AFP/Getty Images (top); p. 43: AP Photo (top), Robert Wagenhoffer/CP Images (bottom).

Produced by Plan B Book Packagers
Editorial: Ellen Rodger
Design: Rosie Gowsell-Pattison
Special thanks to consultant and editor Terrance Cox, adjunct professor, Brock University; Athena P. Madan; Tanya Rutledge; Jon Eben Field; Jim Chernishenko

Library and Archives Canada Cataloguing in Publication
Rodger, Marguerite
Quebec / Marguerite Rodger.
(Canada close up)
ISBN 978-0-545-98905-3
1. Québec (Province)--Juvenile literature.
I. Title. II. Series: Canada close up (Toronto, Ont.)
FC2911.2.R64 2009   j971.4   C2008-906867-X

ISBN-10 0-545-98905-1

6 5 4 3 2 1   Printed in Canada   09 10 11 12 13 14

Contents

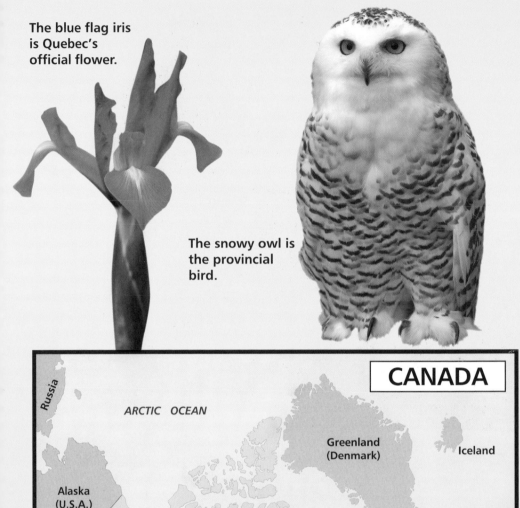

The blue flag iris is Quebec's official flower.

The snowy owl is the provincial bird.

CANADA

Russia

ARCTIC OCEAN

Greenland (Denmark)

Iceland

Alaska (U.S.A.)

ATLANTIC OCEAN

Yukon

Nunavut

Newfoundland and Labrador

Northwest Territories

British Columbia

Hudson Bay

PACIFIC OCEAN

Alberta

Saskatchewan

Manitoba

James Bay

Quebec

Prince Edward Island

Nova Scotia

Ontario

New Brunswick

Lake Huron

Lake Superior

United States

Lake Ontario

Lake Erie

Lake Michigan

Welcome to Quebec!

Quebec is a large and vibrant province. It is also a province of contrasts. It has some of the coldest winters in Canada, and some of the hottest summers. It is the home of many pioneer achievements, such as the *canot de maître*, or Montreal canoe, which transported fur traders from Montreal to Lake Superior. Now it is a centre for cutting-edge research in aerospace technology.

Quebec, with a population of 7.5 million, is the only province in Canada where most people are francophone, or French-speaking. Some Quebecers can trace their roots here back 400 years. Other more recent immigrants have enlivened the province's cities with new cultures and traditions.

Quebec is a province that is committed to remembering its past while working toward its future.

Chapter 1
Forests and Farms

Quebec is Canada's largest province. With an area of 1,667,926 square kilometres, it is three times the size of France! The province spans many different geographic regions, from the northern Arctic to forests, mountains and rich farmlands. Most of the province is covered by the ancient rock of the Canadian Shield.

Long strips of farmland lead down to the St. Lawrence, a remnant of the seigneurial system where land was divided into narrow plots with access to the river.

The Inuit village of Kuujjuaq is located near Ungava Bay. It is the largest village in Nunavik, as Quebec's arctic region is called.

The north

In the far north of the province lies arctic tundra, or frozen treeless ground. About a quarter of the province is tundra. Winters here are cold, dark and long, while the summers are short and cool. South of the tundra is the taiga, a subarctic area of scrubby trees such as black spruce.

Harp seals live in the waters of Ungava Bay.

The James Bay Lowlands

The James Bay Lowlands are in the northwest of the province, at the base of James Bay. This area is a major wetland habitat for birds, including peregrine falcons and loons. It is also home to caribou, moose and black bears.

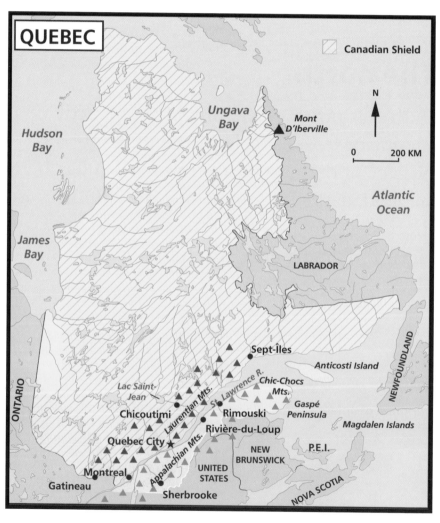

Shield and forest

More than 90 per cent of Quebec's land mass lies within the Canadian Shield. The Canadian Shield is an ancient rock formation covering nearly half of Canada. It stretches from Newfoundland to Alberta and is rich in minerals such as nickel, copper, gold and silver. In north–central Quebec, the Shield is covered with many low hills, rivers, lakes and bogs. Much of the rest of the Canadian Shield is blanketed by forest. The coniferous trees, or evergreens, that grow here provide a home for moose, bears and wolves. Several ancient mountain ranges rise from the Canadian Shield, including the Torngat Mountains near Ungava Bay, the Otish Mountains in central Quebec and the Laurentians in southern Quebec.

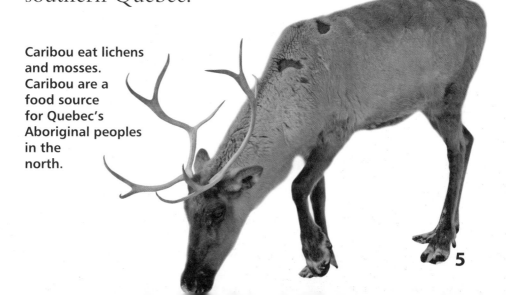

Caribou eat lichens and mosses. Caribou are a food source for Quebec's Aboriginal peoples in the north.

Plains and valleys

The St. Lawrence Lowlands lie south of the Canadian Shield. They extend along both sides of the St. Lawrence River between Quebec City and Montreal, the province's largest cities. Thanks to the St. Lawrence, the third-longest river in Canada, the Lowlands are a centre of business, agriculture and industry.

Millions of years ago, the area was covered by **glaciers**. When the glaciers melted, they left behind a rich soil mixture that's good for farming. Forests of walnut, maple, oak and spruce trees grow here. In the winter, ice storms, blizzards and thick fog are common in the St. Lawrence Lowlands. It can be as cold as -35 degrees Celsius. In the summer, moisture from lakes and rivers nearby creates hot and humid conditions.

Cities and villages

Early Quebec settlers made their homes in areas that had good soil and access to water. As a result, the population of the province is concentrated along the St. Lawrence River.

In the early 1900s, thousands of Quebecers moved north to settle in mining or logging towns. The government also encouraged people to farm these areas, but the land was less fertile.

Quebecers enjoy an outdoor meal at a sidewalk café in Montreal. Half of Quebec's population lives in and around its biggest city.

A ship plies the St. Lawrence River east of Quebec City. The river is a major transportation route between the Atlantic Ocean and the Great Lakes.

Mont Tremblant is a popular ski resort in Quebec's Laurentian Mountains. They are part of the Canadian Shield, one of the world's oldest rock formations.

A boy holds several bunches of carrots freshly picked on his family's organic farm.

From the land

Quebec's farmland has been cultivated for hundreds of years. The original *habitants* grew grain and raised enough animals to feed themselves. Today, many Quebec farmers grow specialty crops and **organic** vegetables and meats. Some farms focus on just one product, such as ducks and geese raised for *foie gras*, a gourmet liver spread.

Water, water everywhere

💧 The name Quebec comes from an Algonquian word meaning "where the river narrows." This refers to the St. Lawrence River near Quebec City.

💧 The St. Lawrence is one of the world's great rivers. It is a major shipping route. And it's full of whales — about 1000 belugas, as well as blue, finback and minke whales. Seals, otters, dolphins and hundreds of species of fish and birds also make the river their home.

💧 There are over one million lakes in Quebec!

💧 The Magdalen Islands are an **archipelago** located in the Gulf of St. Lawrence. These small islands are home to about 13,000 people. Until the early 1900s, they were completely cut off by heavy pack ice in winter. Today the islands are famous for their lobster fishery and as a habitat for seals.

Chapter 2
Je Me Souviens

Quebecers take great pride in their past. The province's motto, *Je me souviens*, which means "I remember," is on the province's coat of arms and every licence plate. People say it means, "I will remember my history and heritage."

Early inhabitants

Evidence shows that ancestors of the Iroquoian- and Algonquian-speaking peoples lived in southern and central Quebec as far back as 8000 years ago. Various peoples have inhabited the far north, now known as Nunavik, for over 4000 years. The Inuit have lived here for hundreds of years, sharing a part of the territory with the Cree people. The Innu live in the northeastern parts of the province.

The Inuit hunted whales and seals, and fished in the Arctic waters. The Algonquian-speaking Cree and Innu were hunters, fishers and gatherers who lived in the rugged regions of the Canadian Shield. They were semi-nomadic, which means they moved often in order to find food. The Iroquois lived in the St. Lawrence Valley, where they fished, hunted and grew crops such as corn and squash.

Today, Aboriginal peoples still live in Quebec and make up one per cent of the province's population. The Inuit live in small villages. Most First Nations peoples live on **reserves** throughout the province.

Many Cree people of northern Quebec still set up summer hunting camps where they hunt and preserve moose meat.

Cartier's claim

The first European explorer to arrive in Quebec was Jacques Cartier. He made three voyages here. On the first, in 1534, he sailed the St. Lawrence River and claimed the land for France. On the second (1535 to 1536), he spent a winter with his ship trapped in ice. On the third (1541 to 1542), he established a **colony** called Charlesbourg–Royal near what is Quebec City today. The colony failed, a victim of disease and attacks by the Iroquois.

At Gaspé, Cartier raised a nine-metre cross to claim the land.

The Father of New France

Samuel de Champlain was an explorer and mapmaker who made several voyages to the **New World**. He endured a brutal winter in what is now Maine, and helped build a settlement called Port Royal in what is now Nova Scotia. He is known as the "Father of New France" because in 1608, he established Quebec, the first permanent settlement in the French colony. With little more than two dozen settlers, Champlain set up a fur trading post. He also formed a relationship with the Montagnais and Huron peoples. Without their help, the settlers would not have survived the harsh winters.

Many statues honour Champlain and his achievements. This one is in Quebec City. In 1608 he wrote in his journal: "I searched for a good place for our habitation but could not find one more convenient or better situated than the point of Quebec."

The colony grows

The French colony grew slowly. To encourage more settlers to move there from France, King Louis XIII established the seigneurial system in 1626. Under this system, land belonged to the king and was managed by landlords called *seigneurs*. The land along the banks of the St. Lawrence River was divided into long, narrow strips with access to water. Farmers known as *habitants* leased the land and paid rent or gave a portion of their crops to their *seigneur* each year.

Artist Cornelius Krieghoff's *The Habitant Farm*, painted in 1856, depicts a scene of everyday life in rural Quebec.

Over time, the number of permanent settlers increased. Around 1642 some went to live in the new settlement of Ville-Marie, which would later become Montreal. In the 1660s, France's King Louis XIV further increased the population by sending hundreds of women to marry the many single soldiers and farmers in New France. These women were known as *les filles du roi* ("the king's daughters") because the king paid their way to New France. The population reached 70,000 by the mid-1700s. But it was still a small colony when compared to the British colonies in the south.

Adventurers and explorers

The story of New France is partly a tale of explorers, adventurers and heroes whose daring actions are part of Quebec **folklore**. The most adventurous were the *coureurs des bois* – fur traders who worked for themselves – and the *voyageurs,* who worked for merchants. Many were *habitants* who left their farms on the St. Lawrence and travelled to Aboriginal communities in the wilderness on fur trading quests.

Voyageurs were licensed traders who worked for trading companies. They were strong men who paddled 10-man *canots de maître* from Montreal to as far away as Saskatchewan and back. Each paddler had to be able to carry 40 kilograms of furs and supplies. They ate a steady diet of salted pork and pemmican, which was dried bison meat and fat. They also endured swarms of biting insects. It was the *coureurs des bois* and *voyageurs* who explored, mapped and applied French names to much of North America.

Voyageurs travelled into the interior of North America, using rivers and lakes as highways. They sang to co-ordinate their paddling and slept under their propped-up canoes.

Constant struggles

From the late 1600s until the mid 1700s, colonists in New France endured many attacks and wars as Britain and France battled over territory in North America. Quebec City was a walled fortress that was constantly under threat. French settlers also had to battle the Iroquois until a **peace treaty** was signed in 1701.

Both James Wolfe, the British general, and the Marquis de Montcalm, the French commander (above), were wounded and died after the battle of the Plains of Abraham.

The Conquest

During the **Seven Years War** (1756–1763) France and Britain once again fought for control of North America. The British took Quebec after the battle of the **Plains of Abraham** in 1759. Montreal fell the following year. At the end of the war in 1763, Britain took possession of France's territories in North America. Quebecers still remember this as the Conquest. Over time, the British realized it would be easier to govern the colony if the people of Quebec were allowed to keep French laws, their language and their **Roman Catholic** religion.

Name that territory!

Keeping track of Quebec's many names and historic territory can be confusing. Originally, Quebec meant the area around the St. Lawrence that Champlain first established in 1608. It was the centre of the colony of New France. Over the years, Quebec's name changed and its territory grew – and shrank. After the Conquest in 1763, it became the province of Quebec. In 1774 it was expanded north to the Labrador coast, west beyond Lake Superior and south to include the Ohio Valley. In 1783 it lost the land below the Great Lakes. In 1791 what remained was divided and became Lower Canada and Upper Canada (Ontario). In 1840 Lower Canada became Canada East. Finally, in 1867, Quebec regained its name and became part of the Dominion of Canada.

Rebellion

In 1837 many colonists in Lower Canada were upset at the way they were being governed by the Château Clique, a group of wealthy businessmen. The *Patriotes*, as the group of colonists was known, demanded changes to the colonial government and more freedoms. When they were ignored, they rebelled. A series of battles left 325 people dead. The *Patriote* leaders were imprisoned or exiled, with 58 transported to Australia as

punishment. This rebellion, and another in Upper Canada at the same time, convinced Britain to examine how its colonies here were ruled.

The *Patriotes* assemble with weapons at a farmhouse.

Modern Quebec has many faces. Most immigrants to the province speak French in addition to one or two other languages.

A land of immigrants

Quebec has a long history as a land of immigrants. In the early 1800s, people arrived from England, Scotland and Ireland. Many settled in Montreal. Canada's first Jewish temple opened in Montreal in 1768. Later, people came from Eastern Europe, Portugal, Greece and Italy. In the last twenty years, many have come to Quebec from Central America, the Middle East, Asia, Africa and from Caribbean countries such as Haiti. Each wave of immigrants has brought something new to the province's culture.

Masters of their own house

Since the birth of Canada, Quebec has struggled to keep the French language and culture alive in a province surrounded by English-speakers. In the 1960s, *la révolution tranquille* (the Quiet Revolution) took place. It was a period of great change in Quebec. The people wanted to be "masters of their own house" and shake off the controlling influence of the church and a rigid provincial government. Quebecers began to direct their own future in education, the economy and culture.

Not long after, in 1970, came the October Crisis, one of Quebec's darkest periods. Members of the *Front de libération du Québec* (FLQ), a group that used violence to demand Quebec independence, kidnapped a British diplomat and a Quebec government minister. The Canadian government brought in soldiers. Four hundred and fifty people suspected of supporting the FLQ were rounded up and held in jail. The FLQ murdered the government minister and, after negotiations, the diplomat was set free.

Children watch as a soldier stands guard near a helicopter at the Quebec Provincial Police headquarters in Montreal during the 1970 October Crisis. The Canadian government brought in the army and gave police more powers to arrest people and hold them in jail, in an effort to find the FLQ kidnappers and those who helped them.

Since the October Crisis, Quebec has worked hard to promote the French language and culture in a positive way. The National Assembly of the provincial legislature declared that Quebec is a nation. In 1980 and 1995, referendums were held in the province, asking voters to decide whether they wanted to become independent from the rest of the country. In 1980, 59 per cent said no. In 1995, 50.58 per cent said no. Quebec remained part of Canada. In 2006, the Canadian government recognized that Quebecers form a nation – but within a united Canada.

"No" supporters gather at a rally before the 1995 referendum. The vote on whether Quebec should remain part of Canada was very close.

Chapter 3
Made in Quebec

Famous for its natural resources, Quebec is now known throughout the world for its high-tech industries such as aircraft manufacturing and computer software. Did you know that 1 in every 200 Quebecers works in the aerospace industry? Aerospace technology is ranked first among the province's exports. This is an industry that designs and produces aircraft and spacecraft.

The Canadarm2 anchors an astronaut to a foot restraint on the International Space Station.

The research and development of pharmaceuticals, or drugs, is also a very important industry. Medicines for the treatment of both AIDS and asthma have been developed in Quebec laboratories.

Video games and animation development account for over 100,000 jobs in Quebec. Award-winning software that has been used in the television and film industries in productions such as *The Simpsons* and *SpongeBob SquarePants* has been developed in Montreal.

Natural resources

Many of Quebec's most important industries still spring from its natural resources. Because forests cover so much of the province, forestry is big business. Quebec is the world's largest exporter of newsprint, as well as a primary producer of Christmas trees in North America.

Tire sur la neige is a maple syrup treat.

A team of horses waits outside a traditional *cabane à sucre*. Here sap collection is done the old-fashioned way. Making maple syrup is both an industry and a tourist attraction.

Quebec is the world's largest producer of maple syrup! Sap is harvested from the province's abundant *érablières* (sugar bushes). In late March and early April, maple syrup harvesters head out to *cabanes à sucre* (sugar shacks) where they boil down the sap to make maple syrup. Quebecers love to pour maple syrup on the snow outdoors and scoop it up with wooden sticks, making *tire sur la neige*, a traditional maple taffy.

Mining is a very important part of Quebec's economy. Copper, zinc, nickel, gold and silver deposits can all be found in the Canadian Shield. The province is the world's fourth-largest producer of aluminum, and the second-largest of magnesium.

29

The James Bay Project is a series of hydroelectic power stations on the La Grande River watershed in northwestern Quebec.

Water power

Fresh water covers 10 per cent of Quebec, making it one of the world's largest fresh water reservoirs. Water is used to produce electricity, and about 97 per cent of the province's power production is **hydroelectric**. Quebec boasts one of the world's largest hydroelectric developments – the La Grande complex near James Bay.

Say cheese!

While much of the north is covered in forest, the southern part of the province is a fertile agricultural region. Farms in the St. Lawrence Lowlands produce fruits, vegetables, livestock and dairy products. Quebec accounts for half of Canada's cheese production. More than 300 different kinds of cheeses are produced in the province. Many of the *fromageries* (cheese factories) are small and make specialty cheeses found nowhere else.

Quebec is known for its fine cheeses made from the milk of cows, sheep and goats.

The walls of Vieux Quebec are four metres thick.

Chapter 4

Old and New

Driving through Quebec, you might notice old stone farmhouses and other historic buildings topped by steeply sloped roofs ending in a curve. This helps prevent roofs collapsing under the heavy snow of Quebec's winters. But architecture isn't the only thing that makes the province **distinctive**. Quebec City, the capital, is one of the oldest walled cities in North America. Montreal is the second-largest French-speaking city in the world, where you might see friends and family *donner un bec* (greet each other with a kiss on each cheek).

Mmm ... poutine and more!

Today, Quebec's foods are as multicultural as its citizens. But Quebecers still occasionally eat hearty traditional dishes such as *tourtière,* a spiced meat pie served on Christmas Eve. Regional dishes are tasty and inventive. *Crevettes de Matane* are small, sweet shrimp caught in the St. Lawrence near Sept-Îles. Blueberries from Lac Saint-Jean and lobsters from the Magdalen Islands and the Gaspé peninsula are a treat. Montreal's Jewish community has made Quebec **cuisine** famous for Montreal-style bagels and smoked meat sandwiches. The most famous Quebec fast food is *poutine* – fries topped with cheese curds and dark gravy. Sold in restaurants and at roadside snack bars, it is now popular throughout Canada.

Quebecers have a sweet tooth too! Maple syrup is plentiful and maple sugar candy and sugar pie are so sweet they can make your teeth ache.

Circus arts

Want to learn how to contort your body or master the trapeze? Head to Montreal and the National Circus School, the only school of its kind in North America that offers diplomas in circus arts. Opened in 1981 to train professional circus performers, many of its graduates now perform at the world's top circuses, including Quebec's own Cirque du Soleil.

Cirque du Soleil is the world's most famous acrobatic circus. It began in Baie-Saint-Paul as a tiny touring act in the late 1980s. Today, the circus has permanent venues in several countries and tours the world with more than a dozen shows.

Cirque du Soleil troupe members wear colourful makeup and fantastic costumes.

Fête nationale is a big holiday. Many Quebecers march each year in parades that celebrate the province.

Celebrating traditions

Quebecers love to get together for parties with family and friends. There are many opportunities to have fun, including the province's biggest holiday, *Fête nationale du Québec*. Celebrated on June 24, it is marked by parades, fireworks and public concerts. It began as Saint-Jean-Baptiste Day, a traditional religious holiday, but has become a celebration of the province.

The *habitants* brought the musical traditions of France to the New World. French-Canadian fiddlers adapted Scottish and Irish **reels** and developed their own style of jaunty tunes to play at dances and weddings. They accompany their playing with a heel-toe-toe foot tapping called clogging. Quebec folk music often includes piano, spoons, jaw harp, accordion and harmonica, as well as the fiddle. Fiddles are a part of some Quebec pop music as well.

Moving day in Quebec is July 1, when rental leases end and thousands of people move on the same day.

Chapter 5

Quebec Is Winter

Cold, snowy winters are so much a part of life in Quebec that many books, poems and plays have been written about the winter season. Movies made in Quebec often feature wintry scenes. And a famous Quebec song says it all: *"Mon pays ce n'est pas un pays, c'est l'hiver."* ("My country isn't a country, it's winter.")

The winters are long – sometimes lasting seven months! – but people make the most of winter sports and activities. Skiers spend days on the hills and at the many resorts in the province. People play hockey in arenas and on outdoor ponds and backyard rinks. Others snowshoe, ski, snowboard, skate and go ice fishing.

Bombardier stands with one of his early snowmobiles, the Muskeg.

Inventing the snowmobile

Another popular winter activity in the province is snowmobiling. Joseph–Armand Bombardier, a Quebec mechanic and inventor, made his first snow machine in 1922 – when he was just fifteen years old!

Bombardier lived in Valcourt, Quebec, east of Montreal. Until the late 1940s, the province did not plough country roads. People were often housebound by metres of snow, or used horse-drawn sleighs to get around.

Bombardier saw the snow as a challenge and an opportunity. By the late 1930s, he had a company that made and sold various kinds of snowmobiles – tractors and troop carriers and passenger vehicles. In 1958 he introduced the "Ski-Dog" – a light machine for fur trappers or anyone else who needed to get around in the snow. This became the Ski-Doo, and a mainstay of winter transportation. Today, Bombardier's company has grown to become a major world producer of snowmobiles, as well as trains and aircraft.

Winter carnival

One of the most important winter traditions in the province is *Carnaval de Québec*, held every February in Quebec City. It's the largest winter carnival in the world. Introduced as its mascot in 1954, *Bonhomme Carnaval* is a smiling snowman who wears a traditional *habitant's* red tuque and sash. Activities and events during the carnival include winter sports, snow and ice sculptures, and dogsled and canoe races on the frozen St. Lawrence River.

Ice canoe races across the St. Lawrence River are a *Carnaval de Québec* event.

Chapter 6
Points of Pride

▶ Quebec is home to the first Canadian to travel to space. Marc Garneau, born in Quebec City, has been aboard three different NASA space shuttle flights. Montreal-born astronaut Julie Payette operated the Canadarm during a 1999 mission.

▶ Montreal was the site of the most successful world's fair of the 20th century. Expo 67 ran for seven months and had 50 million visitors.

► Hockey is so popular in Quebec that some say it is a provincial religion! The Montreal Canadiens, nicknamed the Habs, are the province's only National Hockey League team. Founded in 1909, the Canadiens have won 24 Stanley Cups, more than any other team. Maurice "Rocket" Richard, who played for the Habs from 1942 to 1960, was a team and league legend. He was the first player to score 50 goals in 50 games.

► Singer Céline Dion is one of Quebec's most famous entertainers. Dion, the youngest of fourteen children, grew up in Charlemagne, Quebec. She released her first album at thirteen and then went on to win 5 Grammy Awards and 21 Juno Awards.

Glossary

archipelago: A chain or group of islands

colony: A people or territory ruled by another country

cuisine: A style of cooking, particularly from a specific place

distinctive: Special or notable

folklore: The traditional beliefs, legends and customs of a people

glaciers: Enormous masses of compacted and slowly moving ice

habitants: Early settlers in Quebec from France

hydroelectric: Describes power made from moving or falling water

New World: The western hemisphere, which includes North and South America

organic: Food grown or raised without pesticides or chemical fertilizers

peace treaty: An agreement of peace between two warring groups or nations

Plains of Abraham: A farmer's field on the heights at Quebec City and the site of a battle of the Seven Years War at which the English defeated the French in 1759

reels: Fast dance music played on fiddles

reserves: Designated land set aside for First Nations people to live on

Roman Catholic: Describes a Christian religion headed by the Pope in Rome

Seven Years War: A European war (1756-1763) involving England, France and their allies that spilled over into North America and ended with France losing its colonies in North America